W9-BEY-665

AN ILLUSTRATED DATA GUIDE TO

WORLD WAR II
BOMBERS

Compiled by
Christopher Chant

TIGER BOOKS INTERNATIONAL
LONDON

This edition published in 1997 by
Tiger Books International PLC
Twickenham

Published in Canada in 1997 by
Vanwell Publishing Limited
St. Catharines, Ontario

© Graham Beehag Books
Christchurch
Dorset

Printed in Hong Kong

ISBN 1-85501-858-6

CONTENTS

Avro Type 683 Lancaster

Manufacturer: A.V. Roe & Co. Ltd.

Country of origin: UK

Specification: Lancaster B.Mk III

Type: Heavy bomber

Accommodation: Pilot and co-pilot on the enclosed flightdeck, and navigator/observer, bombardier/gunner, radio operator and two gunners carried in the fuselage

Entered service: Early 1942

Left service: Late 1950s

Armament (fixed): Two 0.303in (7.7mm) Browning trainable forward-firing machine-guns with 1,000 rounds per gun in the power-operated Frazer-Nash F.N.5 nose turret, two 0.303in (7.7mm) Browning trainable machine-guns with 1,000 rounds per gun in the power-operated Frazer-Nash F.N.50 dorsal turret, and four 0.303in (7.7mm) Browning trainable rearward-firing machine-guns with 2,500 rounds per gun in the power-operated Frazer-Nash F.N.20 tail turret

Armament (disposable): Up to 14,000lb (6,350kg) of disposable stores carried in a lower-fuselage weapons bay rated at 14,000lb (6,350kg), and generally comprising one 12,000lb (5,443kg) bomb, or one 8,000lb (3,629kg) and six 500lb (227kg) bombs, or one 4,000lb (1,814kg) and six 1,000lb (454kg) and two 250lb (113kg) bombs, or six 2,000lb (907kg) and three 250lb (113kg) bombs, or six 1,500lb (680kg) mines, or fourteen 1,000lb (454kg) bombs

Operational equipment: Standard communication and navigation equipment, plus optical bomb sight, optical gunsights, H2S nav/attack radar, and F.24 camera

Powerplant: Four Packard (Rolls-Royce) Merlin 28 or 38

A sturdy and capable aeroplane, the Avro Lancaster was Britain's most important heavy night bomber of World War II, and is here seen in the markings of No. 467 Squadron of RAF Bomber Command.

Vee piston engines each rated at 1,460hp (1,089kW) at 6,250ft (1,905m) and 1,435hp (1,070kW) at 11,000ft (3,353m)

Fuel capacity: Internal fuel 2,154 Imp gal (9,792.1 litres) plus provision for up to 800 Imp gal (3,636.8 litres) of auxiliary fuel in one or two 400 Imp gal (1,818.4 litre) weapons-bay tanks; external fuel none

Dimensions: Span 102ft 0in (31.09m); aspect ratio 8.00; area 1,300.00sq ft (120.77sq m); length 68ft 10in (20.98m) with the tail down; height 20ft 4in (6.19m) with the tail down; tailplane span 33ft 0in (10.06m); wheel track 23ft 9in (7.24m)

Weights: Empty 41,000lb (18,597kg) equipped; normal

take-off 68,000lb (30,845kg); maximum take-off 72,000lb (32,659kg)

Performance: Maximum level speed 'clean' 244kt (281mph; 452km/h) at 11,000ft (3,353m) declining to 235kt (271mph; 436km/h) at 6,250ft (1,905m); cruising speed, maximum 197kt (227mph; 365km/h) at optimum altitude and economical 188kt (216mph; 348km/h) at 20,000ft (6,096m); typical range 903nm (1,040 miles; 1,673km) with a weapons load of 10,000lb (4,536kg); climb to 20,000ft (6,096m) in 41min 24sec; service ceiling 24,500ft (7,467m)

Variants

Lancaster Mk I: The most successful and celebrated heavy bomber used by the RA'ís Bomber Command for its night offensive in the second half of World War II (1939-45), the Lancaster was built to the extent of some 7,300 aircraft during the course of the war, but did not actually begin life until the war was already three months old. At that time the Avro company's most important design team, under the supervision of Roy Chadwick, was concerned mostly with the development of the Type 679 Manchester twin-engined bomber that had resulted, like the rival Handley Page H.P.56, from the Air Ministry's P.13/36 requirement for a medium bomber with a powerplant of two Rolls-Royce Vulture X-type engines. The whole P.13/36 programme was troubled by the slow and uncertain development of the Vulture engine, which eventually materialised as a powerful but unreliable type, and as early as 1937 Handley Page had received permission to revise its H.P.56 design with two Vultures to a powerplant of four Rolls-Royce Merlin Vee piston engines, thereby creating the H.P.57 Halifax heavy bomber. The Air Ministry persisted with the twin-Vulture Manchester, however, and plans were laid for the large-scale production of this type by a group of manufacturers that included Avro, Armstrong Whitworth, Fairey and Metropolitan-Vickers.

Chadwick and his design team still had severe reservations about the long-term viability of the Vulture powerplant, however, and initiated several studies for versions of the Manchester with a different powerplant. At the end of 1939, Avro was informed by the Air Ministry that it should proceed with the detail design of the Manchester Mk II (that would be a minimum-change development of the

This pair of Avro Lancasters of No.44 Squadrons reveal the camouflage and markings typical of this bomber, together with the defensive armament grouped in the two-gun nose and dorsal turrets and the four-gun tail turret.

Manchester Mk I with a powerplant of two Napier Sabre H-type piston engines or two Bristol Centaurus radial piston engines), but this project was soon overtaken by that for the Manchester Mk III with a powerplant of four Merlin engines. Despite the change from two to four engines, the Manchester Mk III was seen as a relatively straightforward development that would retain the Manchester Mk I's fuselage, tail unit, and flat wing centre section, which was of the constant-chord type and carried the nacelles that supported the retractable main units of the tailwheel landing gear and would now be adapted for the Merlin engine in place of the original Vulture: to the outer ends of this section would be added new longer-span outer panels that were to be dihedraled, and tapered in thickness and chord, to carry the nacelles for the other pair of Merlin engines.

Avro accorded the new company designation Type 683 to the revised type, and estimated that it would be able to carry a weapons load of 12,000lb (5,443kg) over a range of

868nm (1,000 miles; 1,609km) at a speed of 212kt (244mph; 393km/h) after take-off at a maximum weight of 57,000lb (25,855kg). This estimate suggested that the Type 683 would provide considerably greater capability than the Manchester, even though it would place an additional burden on Merlin production. The Air Ministry thought that the Type 683 would be slightly less capable than the rival H.P.57, but ordered Avro to place the model in production as soon as it had completed its orders for 300 Manchesters.

As the new model made extensive use of existing components and assemblies, the completion of detail design work and the construction of the two prototypes moved ahead rapidly, and the first prototype made its maiden flight in January 1941 as what was clearly a derivative of the Manchester Mk I with its original type of short-span tailplane carrying small endplate vertical surfaces supplemented by a centreline surface, and with a defensive armament of two 0.303in (7.7mm) Browning trainable forward-firing machine-guns in a power-operated Frazer-Nash F.N.5 nose turret and four 0.303in (7.7mm) Browning trainable rearward-firing machine-guns in a power-operated Frazer-Nash F.N.4A tail turret.

After initial flight trials, the first prototype was delivered to the Aircraft & Armament Experimental Establishment at Boscombe Down for official trials. The second prototype was completed for a maiden flight in May 1941 with the tailplane increased in span from 22ft 0in (6.71m) to 33ft 0in (10.06m) and carrying larger endplate vertical surfaces that removed the need for the centreline fin, and with the defensive armament of the first prototype upgraded to the planned production standard: this comprised two 0.303in (7.7mm) Browning trainable forward-firing machine-guns in a power-operated Frazer-Nash F.N.5 nose turret, four 0.303in (7.7mm) Browning trainable rearward-firing

The Avro Lancaster had ample power and a large wing, which facilitated the carriage of an increasingly heavy bomb load in a large lower-fuselage weapons bay or, in the case of single very large loads such as the 22,000lb (9,979kg) 'Grand Slam' penetration bomb, semi-externally under the fuselage.

machine-guns in a power-operated Frazer-Nash F.N.20 tail turret, two 0.303in (7.7mm) Browning trainable machine-guns in the power-operated Frazer-Nash F.N.50 dorsal turret, and two 0.303in (7.7mm) Browning trainable machine-guns in the power-operated Frazer-Nash F.N.64 ventral turret.

The prototypes had a powerplant of four Merlin XX engines each rated at 1,280hp (954kW) for take-off, 1,460hp (1,089kW) at 6,250ft (1,905m) and 1,435hp (1,070kW) at 11,000ft (3,353m), and driving a three-blade de Havilland metal propeller of the constant-speed type. The prototype trials were so successful that the Air Ministry decided to terminate Manchester production immediately, after the delivery of only 200 aircraft, so that construction of the new Lancaster could begin as soon as possible.

The first Lancaster Mk I off the production line flew in October 1941, and on Christmas Eve three aircraft were delivered to No. 44 Squadron for operational trials, which culminated in the type's first operational sorties in March 1942. Deliveries to operational squadrons were not as rapid as had been hoped, for it became apparent that the wingtips required strengthening and a number of other changes needed to be implemented, including a revision of the upper skinning of the wing, but in general the Lancaster Mk I was very similar to the second prototype.

Operational squadrons soon discovered that the ventral turret saw little action and therefore they often removed it, and two officially inspired changes were the addition of a carefully shaped fairing round the lower edge of the dorsal turret to improve the airflow around this protruding feature and also to create a 'taboo track' to prevent the gunner from firing into any part of the airframe, and from the fifth aeroplane an increase in internal fuel capacity from 1,710 Imp gal (7,773.7 litres) in four wing tanks to 2,154 Imp gal (9,792.1 litres) in enlarged standard tanks and additional tanks installed farther outboard in the wings.

The Lancaster Mk I was an immediate operational success, and the fact that the Lancaster was 'right' in all important respects from the very beginning of its service career is attested by the facts that large-scale production saw the delivery of only three more variants (one major and two minor) and that the Lancaster Mk I remained in production until the end of World War II. However, there were considerable developments during the course of each variant's production run: in the Lancaster Mk I, for example, the weapons bay was soon provided with a strengthened support structure for the carriage of a single 8,000lb (3,629kg) bomb, and was then fitted with modified doors to permit the carriage of a single 12,000lb (5,443kg) bomb.

As first delivered with a powerplant of four Merlin XX engines, the Lancaster Mk I had a maximum take-off weight of 61,500lb (27,896kg), a maximum level speed of 249kt (287mph; 462km/h) at 11,500ft (3,505m), and a range of 1,442nm (1,660 miles; 2,671km) with a weapons load of 14,000lb (6,350kg).

The production standard later switched to the Merlin 22 engine for a maximum take-off weight of 63,000lb (28,577kg), a maximum level speed of 234.5kt (270mph; 434km/h) at 19,000ft (5,790m), and a range of 886nm (1,020 miles; 1,641km) with a weapons load of 14,000lb (6,350kg) increasing to 2,128nm (2,450 miles; 3,942km) with a weapons load of 5,500lb (2,495kg).

The production standard later switched again to the Merlin 24 engine rated at 1,640hp (1,223kW) at 2,000ft (610m) and 1,500hp (1,118kW) at 9,500ft (2,895m) for normal and overload maximum take-off weights of 68,000 and 72,000lb (30,845 and 32,659kg) respectively.

Further improvements introduced to the Lancaster Mk I included H2S navigation and bombing radar, introduced in August 1943 on aircraft without the bulged weapons bay and easily distinguishable by the large opaque Perspex fairing over its ventral antenna; and the ability to carry the 22,000lb (9,979kg) 'Grand Slam' transonic penetration bomb in 33 Merlin 24-engined Lancaster B.Mk I (Special) conversions with the weapons bay doors removed and aerodynamic fairings replacing the nose and dorsal turrets that were eliminated to save weight.

Like all other Lancaster variants, the Lancaster B.Mk I was operated solely in the European theatre during World War II. As the end of the war drew near, in the autumn of 1944, thought was given to the use of the Lancaster in support of British operations against the Japanese in the Far East. In its basic form the Lancaster B.Mk I lacked the range for operations in this theatre, so aircraft delivered in 1945 were completed to the Lancaster B.Mk I (FE) standard with a number of tropicalisation features and provision for the installation of a large saddle tank, carrying 1,200 Imp gal (5,455.2 litres) of fuel, between the rear of the flightdeck and the position of the dorsal turret, which was removed. Production of the Lancaster Mk I (from late 1942 Lancaster B.Mk I and after the war Lancaster B.Mk I) totalled 3,434 aircraft.

Lancaster Mk II: Towards the end of 1941, production of the Lancaster Mk I was accelerating so rapidly that there were fears that airframe production would soon outstrip Merlin availability, and consideration was given to a derivative using an engine that was in less demand. The choice fell on the Bristol Hercules radial piston engine in its Hercules VI form, rated at 1,725hp (1,286kW).

The Air Ministry ordered two prototypes of this Lancaster Mk II: the second was not completed, and the first made its maiden flight in November 1941 with a slight lengthening of the weapons bay and the F.N.64 ventral turret. Trials revealed that the Lancaster Mk II closely resembled the Lancaster Mk I in weight and in performance, with the sole exception that the service ceiling was slightly higher than 15,000ft (4,572m). Even so, it was decided to place the model in production, and Armstrong Whitworth delivered 300 examples from September 1942, some of the later aircraft incorporating the bulged weapons bay introduced on later Lancaster Mk Is and the revised powerplant of four Hercules XVI radial engines rated identically to the original Hercules VI engines. The model was soon redesignated as the Lancaster B.Mk II, but production was not as extensive as originally planned as Merlin production did in fact match demand.

Lancaster B.Mk III: Known at the very beginning of its career as the Lancaster Mk III and after World War II as the Lancaster B.Mk 3, this was the direct equivalent of the Lancaster Mk I (Lancaster B.Mk I) with a powerplant of four Merlin engines built under license in the United States by Packard with the local designation V-1650. When used in the Lancaster B.Mk III, these engines were the Merlin 28 or 38 equivalent to the Merlin 22, and the Merlin 224 equivalent to the Merlin 24. The first trial installation of American-built engines was made in a Lancaster Mk I conversion that flew in August 1942, and the first production aircraft became available later in the same year.

Twenty-three examples of the Lancaster Mk III type were adapted for delivery of the 'bouncing bomb', designed by Dr Barnes Wallis for the celebrated attack by No. 617 Squadron in May 1943 on the Eder, Enepe, Lister, Mohne and Sorpe dams. Another special weapon that could be carried by the Lancaster Mk III (and also by the Lancaster Mk I) with the bulged weapons bay designed for the carriage of the 12,000lb (5,443kg) high-capacity blast bomb was the 12,000lb (5,443kg) 'Tallboy', also designed by Barnes Wallis. This was a highly streamlined unit intended to reach supersonic speed before impacting, giving it considerable penetration before detonation: the weapon was used successfully against the battleship KMS *Tirpitz*, deep railway tunnels and similar communications targets, and the concrete roofs of U-boat pens.

Production of the Lancaster B.Mk III totalled 3,030 aircraft, with weights and performance identical with those of their Lancaster Mk I equivalents. Changes effected later in the production run included the general omission of the F.N.64 ventral turret, the frequent replacement of the

The Avro Lancaster remained useful after World War II, this being a Lancaster Mk 10 operated by No.404 Squadron of the Royal Canadian Air Force for the maritime reconnaissance role, in which the Lancaster's reliability and good range were vital assets.

F.N.50 turret in the dorsal position by the F.N.79 or F.N.150 units, and the general replacement of the F.N.20 turret in the tail position by the F.N.121 or F.N.82, the former with four 0.303in (7.7mm) Browning machine-guns and the latter with two 0.5in (12.7mm) Browning machine-guns; the heavier-calibre armament was also used in another turret option, the Rose-Rice Type R No.2 Mk I, that was often combined with another development late in the war, namely the 'Village Inn' Automatic Gun-laying Turret incorporating a radar sight for automatic laying and firing of the turret's guns.

The Lancaster B.Mk III was operated solely in the European theatre during World War II, but in support of British operations against the Japanese in the Far East, Lancaster B.Mk III aircraft delivered in 1945 were completed to the B.Mk III (FE) standard with a number of tropicalisation features and provision for the installation of a large saddle tank, carrying 1,200 Imp gal (5,455.2 litres) of fuel, between the rear of the flightdeck and the position of the dorsal turret, which was removed. Like the Lancaster B.Mk I (FE), the B.Mk III (FE) saw no operational service before the surrender of Japan following the atomic bombings of Hiroshima and Nagasaki in August 1945. The Lancaster Mks IV and V were considerably improved versions that eventually matured after World War II as the Lincoln B.Mks 1 and 2.

Lancaster B.Mk VI: Inspired by the Lancaster Mk IV with a powerplant of four Merlin 85 engines each rated at 1,635hp (1,219kW) and driving a four-blade propeller, this was a development of the Lancaster Mk III with the same powerplant but an otherwise unaltered airframe except for the removal of the nose and dorsal turrets and the fairing of the resulting apertures. The prototype conversion made its maiden flight in the spring of 1944, and there followed another six aircraft. Only four of the aircraft were used operationally by Nos 7 and 635 Squadrons in the electronic warfare role with radar jamming and chaff equipment, and even these were withdrawn in November 1944.

Lancaster B.Mk VII: Built to the extent of 180 aircraft that saw service only after the end of World War II, and mostly in the Far East, this was a development of the Lancaster Mk III with a Martin dorsal turret. This power-operated unit was fitted with two 0.5in (12.7mm) Browning trainable machine-guns and was installed further forward on the fuselage than the Frazer-Nash turret.

Lancaster B.Mk X: This designation was accorded to 430 examples of the Lancaster B.Mk III built in Canada by Victory Aircraft, and was identical to the Lancaster B.Mk III in all major respects.

During the course of World War II, the Lancaster flew some 156,000 sorties and dropped 608,612 tons of bombs while operated by a total of 61 squadrons. The last production aeroplane was delivered in February 1946, and although the type remained in service after the war with a total of 14 squadrons (eight based at home and six in the Middle East) it was soon replaced in home service by the Lincoln, and was adapted for tasks such as air/sea rescue and maritime reconnaissance (four squadrons) and photographic survey (one squadron). The last Lancaster was retired from British service in February 1954, but the type remained in French naval air arm service for a period.

A *Gift* for you!

ALEX

into the ocean areas off the USA's eastern and western coasts to detect and destroy hostile fleets and their supporting ships. Boeing realised that the resulting competition, which called for the delivery of a flying prototype by August 1935, would develop into a hard-fought battle between the major companies in the American aircraft industry, and therefore sought a comfortable edge over its rivals in a type that could prove a very profitable production exercise.

Boeing had already developed its Models 214 and 246 for limited production as the B-9 series of twin-engined bombers, and fully appreciated that such a monoplane layout offered little scope for improvement in its twin-engined form, given the relative lack of power available from current radial piston engines or those of the immediate future.

The design team therefore chose to construe the USAAC's multi-engined specification as meaning more than one engine but not necessarily only two engines. The design team decided that a three-engined powerplant, with the third engine on the nose, was impractical as this location would be better employed for the bombardier's position and defensive armament, and therefore concluded that a four-engined powerplant would generate significant advantages. The use of such a powerplant inevitably meant a larger and more expensive airframe, but as the weapons load was restricted to that which could be carried by twin-engined rivals, there was the possibility of higher power/weight and

The condensation trails of the Boeing B-17's quartet of Wright R-1820 engines were typical of the Flying Fortress's cruising regime at high altitude.

power/drag ratios. This combination offered considerable advantages in terms of overall performance (especially in speed, service ceiling and range) and had the additional benefit of providing greater reliability for long overwater flights. The design team began work on the Model 299 in June 1934, and construction of the prototype began in August, at the start of a programme that was to produce one of the most important warplanes of all time. Meanwhile, Boeing was also at work on the Model 294 (XBLR-1, later XB-15) bomber prototype, and the Model 299 can be regarded as an aerodynamic and structural cross between the Model 247 transport and the Model 294 bomber. From the former originated the basic structural design and from the latter came the disposition of the four-engined powerplant, the circular-section fuselage, and the arrangement of the crew, weapons and other military equipment within the fuselage. In terms of size the Model 299 was about midway between the Model 247 and the Model 294, and its span was only 8ft 3in (2.51m) greater than that of its most significant rival, the military derivative of the Douglas DC-3 transport that was designed as the DB-1 and developed into the B-18 Bolo bomber.

Basically, the Model 299 was of all-metal construction with the crew and bomb load accommodated in the forward two-thirds of the fuselage, a conventional but fully cantilevered tail unit with plain control surfaces and a vertical surface that was located well behind the horizontal surface, a low-set wing carrying the fuel tanks, the four engine nacelles on its leading edges and a combination of inboard flaps and outboard ailerons on its trailing edges, and tailwheel landing gear including a tail unit that semi-retracted into the rear fuselage and main units that retracted into the inboard engine nacelles leaving the lower part of each wheel exposed.

As the Model 299 had been conceived as an aerial coast-defence fort, Boeing registered the name Flying Fortress for the type: this was later accepted by the US Army Air Forces (USAAF), as the USAAC had become, and it gradually came to be believed that the name referred to the bomber's defensive capability rather than the offensive power for which it had originally been named.

The Model 299 prototype was a company-owned aeroplane, and made its first flight in July 1935 with a powerplant of four Pratt & Whitney R-1690-S1E-G Hornet radial piston engines each rated at 750hp (559kW), a crew of eight (two pilots, bombardier, navigator/radio operator and four gunners), an offensive load of 4,800lb (2,177kg) carried internally, and a defensive armament of five 0.3in (7.62mm) Browning trainable machine-guns in a small nose turret and in four blister fairings (one dorsal, one ventral and two beam positions). The Model 299 displayed a maximum level speed of 205kt (236mph; 380km/h) and a range of 2,693nm (3,101 miles; 4,990km) at weights that rose from an empty equipped figure of 21,657lb (9,824kg) to a maximum take-off figure of 38,053lb (17,261kg).

Unfortunately, this prototype was lost in October 1935 when a USAAC pilot took off with the controls locked, but by this time the Model 299 had displayed such outstanding performance that in January 1936 the USAAC placed a contract for 13 examples of the improved Model 299B for service trials under the designation YB-17 (later changed to Y1B-17). Delivered between January and August 1937, these aircraft were externally indistinguishable from the Model 299 apart from the revised powerplant of four Wright R-1820-39 radial piston engines each rated at 1,000hp (746kW) for take-off and 850hp (634kW) at 5,000ft (1,524m). There were a number of internal changes, including a switch to a six-man crew and provision for a weapons load of up to 8,000lb (3,629kg). At weights that increased from an empty figure of

24,465lb (11,097kg) to a maximum take-off figure of 42,600lb (19,323kg), the Y1B-17 recorded a maximum level speed of 222kt (256mph; 412km/h) at 14,000ft (4,267m) and a range of 1,196nm (1,377 miles; 2,216km). One of the 13 aircraft was used for technical trials, but the others were delivered to the 2nd Bombardment Group based at Langley Field in Virginia, and were used for operational trials. At the end of the trials programme, the Y1B-17s received the revised designation B-17 indicating their change from service trials to service deployment.

At the time that it ordered the 13 Y1B-17 service test aircraft, the USAAC ordered a fourteenth airframe for static tests. When one of the Y1B-17s was caught in a violent aerial storm and emerged without damage, the service took this as confirmation of the Model 299's structural strength and ordered the completion of the static-test airframe as the Y1B-17A service test aeroplane. Boeing assigned its Model 299F designation to this aeroplane, which was used for the development of a turbocharged engine installation. One Moss/General Electric turbocharger was initially installed above each engine, but this was later changed to the position below each engine that became standard for all B-17s. The R-1820-51 turbocharged engine of this model was rated at 800hp (596kW) at 25,000ft (7,620m) compared to the R-1820-39's best high-altitude rating of 775hp (578kW) at 14,000ft (4,267m) in the Y1B-17: this boosted the Y1B-17A's maximum level speed to 270kt (311mph; 500km/h) at 25,000ft (7,620m) and its service ceiling to well over 30,000ft (9,145m).

The success of the Y1B-17/B-17 paved the way for the first true production variant but, somewhat paradoxically, slowed the service debut of the type in large numbers. The cause of this delay was the USAAC's claim that the new bomber made it the primary means of defending the American coastlines. This role was claimed by the US Navy, however, and the disagreement that broke out between the two services made it difficult for the USAAC to secure adequate funding for the new bomber, whose early models could therefore be built only in small numbers. Boeing at first called the initial production variant the Model 299E but, after a number of changes had been imposed by the USAAC, designated it the Model 299M. In external detail the Model 299M differed from the Model 299B only in its rudder of greater area, larger trailing-edge flaps, and revised nose in which the greenhouse gun turret and ventral bombardier window were eliminated in favour of a simplified glazed section incorporating an optically flat bomb-aiming panel in its lower portion.

Internally, however, the Model 299M differed from its predecessor more significantly in a switch from pneumatically to hydraulically operated brakes and in a redistribution of the crew positions. The Model 299M had the same offensive and defensive armament as the YIB-17, and its other details included a powerplant of four R-1820-51 radial engines each rated at 1,200hp (895kW) for take-off; span of 103ft 9.4in (31.63m) with an area of 1,420.00sq ft (131.92sq m); length of 67ft 9in (20.65m); height of 18ft 4in (5.59m); empty, normal take-off and maximum take-off weights of 27,652, 37,997 and 46,178lb (12,543, 17,235 and 20,946kg) respectively, and maximum level speed of 254kt (292mph; 470km/h) at 25,000ft (7,620m).

The first Model 299M flew in June 1939, and all 39 aircraft (built in six batches as a result of procurement difficulties) were delivered to the USAAC between July 1939 and March 1940 for service with the designation B-17B.

B-17C Flying Fortress: Experience with the B-17 and B-17B paved the way for the B-17C that Boeing built with the company designation Model 299H. The fact that the B-17 was considered an important warplane is reflected by the fact that, while production was limited to a mere 38 aircraft, these were all built in a single batch under one procurement order. The primary changes between the B-17B and the B-17C were in the latter's defensive arrangements: armour protection was added for the crew, self-sealing fuel tanks were introduced, and extensive revision was effected in the offensive and defensive armament.

In this last capacity, the weapons load was increased to a maximum of 10,500lb (4,763kg), and the defensive scheme was changed to one 0.3in (7.62mm) and six 0.5in (12.7mm) trainable machine-guns arranged in a different defensive pattern: the lateral gun blisters were replaced by single-gun waist positions, the ventral gun blister was replaced by a metal 'bathtub' fairing with two machine-guns, the single nose gun was replaced by two cheek guns, the strength of the forward dorsal position was doubled to two guns, and the rear dorsal position carried the single 0.3in (7.62mm) weapon.

The first of these B-17C aircraft flew in July 1940, and all the aircraft had been delivered by November of that year.

Early models of the Boeing B-17, such as the B-17C illustrated here, differed radically from the full-production models in their different tail unit, much inferior defensive armament, and combination of large lateral windows and a ventral gondola.

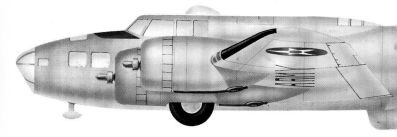

Other details of the B-17C, which was the fastest of all B-17 variants, included a powerplant of four R-1820-64 radial engines each rated at 1,200hp (895kW) for take-off and 1,000hp (746kW) at 25,000ft (7,620m); span of 103ft 9.4in (31.63m) with an area of 1,420.00sq ft (131.92sq m); length of 67ft 11in (20.70m); height of 18ft 4in (5.59m); empty and maximum take-off weights of 29,021 and 47,242lb (13,164 and 21,429kg) respectively; maximum level speed of 281kt (324mph; 521km/h) at 25,000ft (7,620m); cruising speed of 201kt (231mph; 372km/h) at optimum altitude; range of 2,084nm (2,400 miles; 3,862km) with a bomb load of 4,000lb (1,814kg); initial climb rate of 1,300ft (396m) per minute; climb to 10,000ft (3,048m) in 7min 6sec, and service ceiling of 36,000ft (10,973m).

By the time the B-17C was becoming available, the United Kingdom was in desperate need of greater offensive capability as it struggled as the only Western European opponent still facing Germany in World War II, and the USAAC released 20 examples of its small B-17C force to the RAF with the designation Fortress Mk I to which Boeing gave the company designation Model 299U. The USAAC saw this diminution of its strength as a way of gaining information about the B-17's combat capabilities, and the aircraft were ferried to Britain in the spring of 1941. After minimum modifications to include British radio and other equipment, the aircraft were committed to operational missions from July to September 1941 in the hands of No. 90 Squadron of RAF Bomber Command. The aircraft were unwisely used on individual daylight missions at very high altitude, and in 51 missions managed to bomb on only 25 occasions.

It became clear that the B-17C/Fortress Mk I was still an ineffective weapon as a result of difficulties with the Norden bomb sight, many technical problems and failures, the tendency of the guns to freeze at high altitude, the lack of tail defence, and a liability to burn after the fuel tanks had been hit. The British decided that the Fortress was unsuitable for European operations and, after a temporary diversion of four aircraft to the Middle East, from October 1942 the surviving aircraft were entrusted to the maritime reconnaissance role in the hands of Nos 206 and 220 Squadrons of RAF Coastal Command.

B-17D Flying Fortress: Built to the extent of 42 aircraft with the same Boeing model number, this was an improved version of the B-17C and externally distinguishable from its predecessor only by the introduction of cowling flaps. Internally there were a number of changes, including a revised electrical system and a further revision of the accommodation to allow a crew of 10 rather than nine men. The aircraft were ordered in 1940, and all the aircraft were delivered in 1941 after the first machine had made its maiden flight in February of that year. The 18 B-17C aircraft remaining in the United States were converted to the same standard and given the B-17D designation.

These 60 aircraft were the most modern bombers available to the USAAF when the Japanese attack on Pearl Harbor in December 1941 drew the United States into World War II, and many of the aircraft were lost in the opening hours of the Japanese onslaught: 18 of the 33 aircraft operated from Clark and Del Monte Fields in the

Philippines by the 19th Bombardment Group were lost on the ground in the first attack, and the same fate befell most of the aircraft on Hickam Field in Hawaii, where another 12 received varying degrees of damage as they arrived (without armament) from California. The surviving aircraft in the Philippines, which included 16 B-17D aircraft at Del Monte Field, then became the first US aircraft to undertake offensive operations in World War II when they started to raid Japanese shipping north of the Philippines. By the end of December 1941, however, the 19th Bombardment Group was no longer effective and had been withdrawn to Australia for rest and re-equipment before resuming operations against the Japanese in January 1942, when the bombers attacked the Japanese invasion forces on Java in the Netherlands East Indies.

B-17E Flying Fortress: This was the first major production variant of the Flying Fortress family, and resulted directly from the lessons of air operations over Europe in the opening campaigns of World War II. The revised type was known to the manufacturer as the Model 299O, and its most important changes from the Model 299H (B-17C and B-17D) were a completely revised rear fuselage carrying larger tail surfaces (including a differently shaped vertical surface based on that evolved for the later examples of the Model 307 Stratoliner commercial, itself a transport derivative of the Model 299), improved armour protection, a number of internal enhancements, and revised defensive armament. This last change was particularly important: the waist positions were simplified, power-operated Sperry turrets each armed with two 0.5in (12.7mm) machine-guns

The Boeing B-17E was the first Flying Fortress variant with the definitive and considerably larger tail unit as well as better defensive armament including a Sperry ball turret in the ventral position for protection against attack from below.

were added in the dorsal and ventral positions, and a manually operated tail turret was provided for a further pair of 0.5in (12.7mm) machine-guns.

The first B-17E flew in September 1941, and the initial 112 aircraft off the production line featured a ventral turret that was remotely controlled from a periscopic sight in a Plexiglas blister located several feet farther to the rear: in the remaining aircraft this installation was replaced by a Sperry ball turret accommodating a gunner.

The first B-17E bombers were delivered to the 7th Bombardment Group that joined the 19th Bombardment Group in the Pacific theatre from December 1941, and others of the 512 aircraft were allocated to the units that formed the first elements of the 8th Army Air Force in Britain from May 1942. The first British-based unit to become operational with the B-17E was the 97th Bombardment Group, which flew its first mission over occupied Europe in August 1942. Other medium-range raids, mainly to targets in occupied North-West Europe, followed into the early part of 1943, but much of the European-based B-17E strength was diverted from October 1942 to create the striking element of the new 12th Army Air Force that was to support the Anglo-American landing in North-West Africa and the subsequent campaign up to the final elimination of the Axis forces from Africa by May 1943.

The major details of the B-17E included a powerplant of four R-1820-65 radial piston engines each rated at 1,200hp

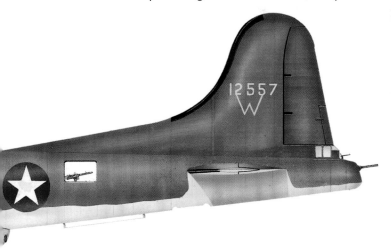

(895kW) for take-off and 1,000hp (746kW) at 25,000ft (7,620m); internal fuel capacity of 2,073.4 Imp gal (9,425.6 litres); span of 103ft 9.4in (31.63m) with an area of 1,420.00sq ft (131.92sq m); length of 73ft 1.5in (22.29m); height of 19ft 2.4in (5.85m); empty, normal take-off and maximum take-off weights of 33,279, 48,726 and 53,000lb (15,095, 22,102 and 24,041kg) respectively; maximum level speed of 276kt (318mph; 512km/h) at 25,000ft (7,620m); maximum cruising speed of 195kt (224mph; 360km/h) at 15,000ft (4,572m); economical cruising speed of 139kt (160mph; 257km/h) at 5,000ft (1,524m); maximum range of 2,866nm (3,300 miles; 5,310km); typical range of 1,737nm (2,000 miles; 3,218km) with a bomb load of 4,000lb (1,814kg); climb to 10,000ft (3,048m) in 7min 6sec, and service ceiling of 36,600ft (11,155m).

Some 45 B-17E bombers were transferred to the RAF from the autumn of 1942 for use by Coastal Command with the designation Fortress Mk IIA and, with the newer B-17F that had been delivered to the RAF earlier than the B-17E to receive the designation Fortress Mk II, served with four maritime reconnaissance and four meteorological reconnaissance squadrons.

B-17F Flying Fortress: Whereas the B-17E resulted from assessment of information reaching the United States about non-American air operations over Europe in the early campaigns of World War II, the B-17F resulted from direct American experience, in this instance with the B-17D against the Japanese in the Pacific and South-West Pacific theatres. The B-17F was externally identifiable from the B-17E only in its use of single-piece blown rather than multi-piece built-up Plexiglas nose transparency; but, in fact, the variant incorporated more than 400 small but collectively important changes that made the B-17F a considerably more formidable warplane than its predecessor.

These changes were added incrementally throughout the B-17F's production life, and included improved armour protection; provision for external bomb racks under the wings increasing the maximum bomb load to 20,800lb (9,435kg) for short-range missions; additional ball-and-socket machine-gun mounts in the nose and the radio compartment for an extra three 0.5in (12.7mm) trainable machine-guns; an electronic link between the Norden bomb sight and the autopilot; changed control settings; more photographic equipment; a revised oxygen system; upgraded main landing gear units allowing an increase in maximum take-off weight to 65,000lb (29,484kg) and eventually to 72,000lb (32,659kg); a dual braking system; self-sealing oil tanks; extra electrical power generation capability; dust filters over the carburettor air inlets; provision for 909.3 Imp gal (4,133.7 litres) of auxiliary fuel in 'Tokyo tanks' installed in the wings; and paddle-blade propellers for the R-1820-97 radial piston engines that were installed in revised nacelles to allow the full feathering of the wider-chord propeller blades.

The other major details of the B-17F included a powerplant of four R-1820-97 radial piston engines each rated at 1,200hp (895kW) for take-off and 1,000hp (746kW) at 25,000ft (7,620m); internal fuel capacity of 2,098.4 Imp gal (9,539.2 litres) that could be supplemented by the auxiliary fuel in 'Tokyo tanks'; span of 103ft 9.4in (31.63m) with an area of 1,420.00sq ft (131.92sq m); length of 74ft 8.9in (22.78m); height of 19ft 2.4in (5.85m); empty, normal take-off and initial maximum take-off weights of 35,728, 48,720 and 56,500lb (16,206, 22,099 and 25,628kg) respectively; maximum level speed of 282kt (325mph; 523km/h) at 25,000ft (7,620m) declining to 260kt (299mph; 481km/h) at 25,000ft (7,620m) in the later aircraft with increased maximum take-off weights; maximum cruising speed of 195kt (224mph; 360km/h) at 15,000ft (4,572m); economical cruising speed of 139kt (160mph; 257km/h) at 5,000ft (1,524m); maximum range of 3,838nm (4,420 miles; 7,113km) with auxiliary fuel; typical range of 1,389nm (1,600 miles; 2,575km) with a bomb load of 6,000lb (2,722kg); climb to 20,000ft (6,096m) in 25min 42sec, and service ceiling of 37,500ft (11,430m).

The initial B-17F flew in May 1942, just two days after the delivery of the last B-17E, and was the first Flying Fortress to be built in the block system adopted by the USAAF in 1942 to differentiate minor improvements of standard introduced on the production line but not meriting a change in the basic letter suffix. Production totalled 3,405 aircraft in the form of 2,300 from Boeing in 28 blocks, 605 from Douglas in 18 blocks, and 500 from Lockheed's Vega subsidiary in 11 blocks. The B-17F was allocated initially to the 8th Army Air Force in Europe, and flew the first American bombing mission against a target in Germany during January 1943. Thereafter the B-17F became the mainstay of the steadily increasing US daylight bombing effort, but operations from mid-1943 revealed

The final and fully definitive model of Boeing's Flying Fortress heavy day bomber was the B-17G, which was essentially the B-17F with the nose revised for the incorporation of a chin turret to provide a defence against the head-on attack that the Germans had discovered to be best against the B-17F.

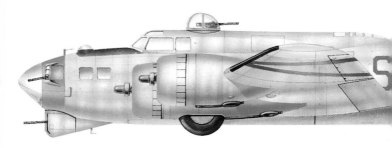

that the Germans were becoming wise to American tactics and also to the defensive limitations of the B-17F against head-on attack.

Some 19 B-17F bombers were transferred to the RAF from the middle of 1942 for use by Coastal Command with the designation Fortress Mk II and, with the older B-17E that was delivered to the RAF later than the B-17F to receive the designation Fortress Mk IIA, served with four maritime reconnaissance and four meteorological reconnaissance squadrons.

B-17G Flying Fortress: This model resulted directly from the experience of the US bomber crews in 1943, which revealed that the B-17F lacked adequate defence against head-on fighter attack. The primary change in the B-17G was therefore the introduction of a power-operated Bendix chin turret armed with two 0.5in (12.7mm) machine-guns, and controlled remotely from the glazed nose position that was now a more practical unit as it lost the one or two manually operated 0.5in (12.7mm) machine-guns that had been fitted in the B-17F. These weapons had not enjoyed adequate fields of fire to be truly effective, and had also made movement in the nose position very difficult.

Other changes effected successively in the B-17G were an improved navigator position; refinement of the bomb-control system; electric rather than hydraulic control of the turbochargers; improved turbochargers; an emergency oil

maximum range 5,063nm (5,830 miles; 9,382km) with auxiliary fuel; typical range 2,822nm (3,250 miles; 5,230km); climb to 20,000ft (6,096m) in 38min 0sec; service ceiling 31,850ft (9,708m)

Variants

B-29 Superfortress: The B-29 is generally remembered as the only warplane to have dropped nuclear weapons in anger, the two instances happening on 6 and 9 August 1945 when the Japanese cities of Hiroshima and Nagasaki were destroyed. The enormous impact of these single events finally persuaded the Japanese authorities to bring the Pacific War (1941-45) of World War II to a speedy conclusion, by agreeing to an unconditional surrender rather than facing the threat of further bombings and/or an American invasion of the Japanese home islands. Yet by the time its A-bombings of Hiroshima and Nagasaki brought an end to the war, the B-29 had effectively neutralised Japan's war-making potential by burning the heart out of her cities, destroying her communications network, crippling her industries, and mining her coastal waters. By any criterion, therefore, the B-29 must be judged one of the most decisive weapons of World War II despite the fact that it entered service only in the later part of 1943 and made its first combat sortie only in June 1944.

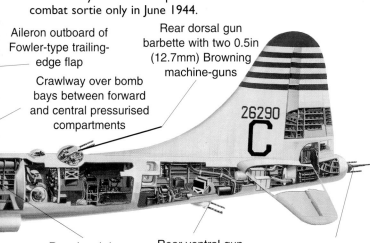

Aileron outboard of Fowler-type trailing-edge flap

Rear dorsal gun barbette with two 0.5in (12.7mm) Browning machine-guns

Crawlway over bomb bays between forward and central pressurised compartments

Rear bomb bay

Rear ventral gun barbette with two 0.5in (12.7mm) Browning machine-guns

Pressurised tail gun compartment with one 20mm cannon and two 0.5in (12.7mm) Browning machine-guns

Twin-wheel retractable main landing gear unit

The origins of this potent bomber can be found in 1938 when Major General Oscar Westover, commanding the USAAC, decided that a new bomber would be needed to supplant the Boeing Model 299 (B-17 Flying Fortress) that was still being evolved through a number of small procurement orders as a result of Congressional parsimony. Westover was killed in an air crash shortly after setting in motion the process that led eventually to the design of the Boeing Model 345. Reflecting Congressional reservations, the Department of War reacted negatively to Westover's official requirement for a 'super bomber', but the project was kept alive by Brigadier General H. H. 'Hap' Arnold, Westover's successor, and by Major General Oliver Echols of the procurement executive. Westover, Arnold and Echols might have been out of step with Congress and with the mainstream of War Department thinking, but were merely following in the well-established pattern of air corps thinking that had begun with Brigadier General William 'Billy' Mitchell in the period immediately following World War I (1914-18).

Although official interest in long-range bombing had apparently declined after the court martial of Mitchell and the bitter quarrels of the later 1920s between the US Army and the US Navy about heavy bombing, far-sighted officers had kept alive the concept of long-range strategic bombing. In April 1934 the USAAC had issued its requirement for a 'Long Range Airplane Suitable for Military Purposes', and Boeing and Martin had each tendered a design for a bomber able to operate from bases in the continental USA against enemy landings in remote areas such as Alaska and Hawaii, and for attacks on enemy naval forces and their supporting elements in deep ocean waters well away from US coasts.

The Boeing Model 294 was declared winner over the Martin design, and a single XBLR-1 (later XB-15) prototype was ordered to provide experience in the design, construction and operation of a long-range bomber able to deliver a substantial weapons load over a range of some 4,342nm (5,000 miles; 8,047km). Although the XB-15 and B-17 Flying Fortress were conceived essentially as tactical bombers, the USAAC had not lost sight of its original conviction that the future of air power lay with the strategic bomber, and this resulted in Westover's requirement for a Very Heavy Bomber (which had become a Very Long Range Bomber by 1940). Initial progress was slow, for there was no official funding available and Boeing had to rely on its own

The Boeing B-29 Superfortress was based on a low-drag design with a circular-section fuselage, a mid-set wing and powerful engines supplied from massive fuel tankage for high speed and very long range with a substantial bomb load.

resources to pay for conceptual planning that reflected the USAAC's evolving requirement: this was based on the use of a large aeroplane with pressurised accommodation for the delivery of a very large weapons load over great range, and at an altitude high enough to offer significant drag reductions in the cruise and a relative immunity to interception by enemy fighters in the attack.

Other features that were adopted at this time included a comparatively small wing and, despite the company's experience with the Model 307 Stratoliner pressurised airliner, pressurisation limited to the crew compartments rather than the whole fuselage. So far as the wing was concerned, the company's initial concept had been to use a moderately large unit carrying a powerplant of four Pratt & Whitney liquid-cooled engines buried in the wings: this would have generated a substantial drag penalty, however, and the company's design team therefore opted for a smaller wing carrying Wright air-cooled radial engines in low-drag nacelles. And so far as the accommodation was concerned, the design team opted for a large pressurised compartment in the nose for the flight and mission crew, a smaller compartment to the rear of the weapons bays for the gunners controlling the dorsal and ventral defensive guns, and a diminutive compartment at the extreme tail for the rear gunner; the forward and central compartments were linked by a crawl tunnel over the weapons bays.

Boeing's first definitive design, evolved via the Model 316, Model 322 and Model 333 plans, was the Model 334 with pressurised accommodation and fully retractable tricycle landing gear, together with a projected maximum take-off weight in the order of 48,000lb (21,773kg). Further revisions led to the Model 334A and then to the Model 341 of which the company built a detailed mock-up in December 1939. In the following month the USAAC released its first true requirement for a 'super bomber' with a speed of 347kt (400mph; 644km/h) and the ability to deliver a weapons load of 2,000lb (907kg) over a radius of 2,314nm (2,665 miles; 4,289km) or a significantly heavier bomb load over a shorter distance. This Requirement 40B was almost immediately revised to reflect the lessons of early air operations over Europe in World War II, and now demanded improved operational features such as heavier defensive armament, self-sealing fuel tanks, and armour protection for the crew and vital systems. The revised requirement was issued in February 1940 and called for a 'Hemisphere Defence Weapon' able to carry a maximum weapons load of 16,000lb (7,258kg).

The Model 341 design had been planned for the carriage of a 2,000lb (907kg) bomb load over a radius of 3,040nm (3,500 miles; 5,633km) at a maximum speed of 352kt

The Boeing B-29's crew had good fields of vision from the extensively glazed hemispherical nose (flight crew) and sighting blisters (defensive gunners

(405mph; 652km/h) after take-off at a maximum weight of 84,000lb (38,102kg), and therefore could not satisfy the 'Hemisphere Defence Weapon' requirement. The Boeing design team accordingly revised the Model 341 into the Model 345 whose estimated performance met all the USAAC's requirements except in speed, which was estimated at 332kt (382mph; 615km/h), but at the expense of a further increase in maximum take-off weight to 120,000lb (54,432kg). Boeing submitted the Model 345 design to the USAAC in May 1940, when Consolidated, Douglas and Lockheed also made their XB-32, XB-31 and XB-30 submissions. The Douglas and Lockheed designs were soon eliminated, and in the final competition between Boeing and Consolidated the decision went to the former's Model 345.

In June 1940 Boeing received a small initial contract for further design work and the wind tunnel testing of models, and during September the USAAC ordered three XB-29 prototypes (one for static tests and two for flight trials) before revising its order in December to demand the construction of three flying prototypes. Boeing started work on the mock-up of the XB-29 in May 1941, and later in the same month the USAAC announced its intention of ordering 250 B-29 bombers to be built in new government-funded facilities at Boeing's plant in Wichita, Kansas. The contract for these 250 aircraft was signed in September 1941, by which time the USAAC had become the USAAF, and the order was increased to 500 aircraft in January 1942, the month after the Japanese attack on Pearl Harbor had drawn America into World War II. Just one month later the programme for the new bomber had acquired so high a priority that the US authorities decided that additional production facilities would be created at government-owned plants to be run by Bell at Marietta in Georgia, by North American at Kansas City, and by the Fisher Body Division of the General Motors Corporation at Cleveland in Ohio. In the event, the last two plants did not produce the B-29: the USAAF traded the Kansas City facility to the US Navy in exchange for the latter's Boeing-run facility at Renton in Washington, and Martin at Omaha in Nebraska replaced the Fisher Body Division so that the latter could concentrate of the production of B-29 assemblies.

The aeroplane that emerged from this effort was a truly prodigious achievement, but was not without its critics. Adverse comment was centred primarily on the bomber's

With the exception of the manned tail position with its one 20mm cannon and two 0.5in (12.7mm) machine guns or three 0.5in (12.7mm) machine guns, the defensive armament of the Boeing B-29 Superfortress was based on power-operated barbettes sighted and remotely controlled from nearby blister glazings via a sophisticated fire-control system. The engines were each fitted with two turbochargers for the maintenance of high power up to very high altitude.

high wing loading, which in turn resulted from the USAAC's initial demands for additional fuel, bomb load, defensive armament and protection. This made the Model 345 the world's heaviest aeroplane at the time of its conception and development, and the very high wing loading prompted USAAF planners to recommend an increase in wing span and area to reduce the loading and therefore the landing speed, which was estimated at some 139kt (160mph; 257km/h) – about double that of the B-17.

Boeing countered with the argument that such an increase would degrade overall performance by increasing weight and drag, and that field performance would be adequate as a result of the incorporation of Fowler flaps along the wing trailing edges inboard of the ailerons: these flaps improved the wing's lift coefficient during take-off and landing, and when extended added some 20 per cent to the wing area and thereby reduced the wing loading to an acceptable figure.

As these arguments were being resolved in Boeing's favour, the company was pressing ahead with construction of the XB-29 prototypes to an exceptionally sleek design based on an all-metal structure employing thick skins that were bolted rather than riveted together to provide the combination of low drag and high strength. In many ways the construction of the airframe was the simplest part of the

performance and could be an important weapon. The type was beset by a host of technical problems, however, and many of them stemming from the fact that the B-29 had been rushed into production before all its problems had been diagnosed and cured.

The USAAF decided that construction of the B-29 initial production model should not be hindered to allow these problems to be dealt with, so as each of the early aircraft was completed from assemblies and components delivered from points all over the United States, it was moved to a special facility at Salina in Kansas, where a force of 600 highly skilled Boeing technicians and USAAF personnel fought the so-called Battle of Kansas (a six-week period in March and April 1944) to make the aircraft capable of undertaking operational service: the first 175 aircraft delivered to Salina had more than 9,900 faults, but the number of faults declined as the lessons of the Battle of Kansas were fed back to the factories and were incorporated at the production stage.

Even so, the B-29 was a formidable proposition for the USAAF, both to introduce into service and also to develop into an effective warplane. Inexperienced crews found the aeroplane difficult to handle and to fly accurately, but with increasing experience came greater capability. The lessons of making all the subsystems work effectively in the extreme cold of flight at 33,000ft (10,058m) were digested, and between January and March 1944 the B-29 crews doubled the range they could achieve on a given quantity of fuel.

Given the B-29's great range with a useful warload, the USAAF decided that the type should be deployed not in Europe against the Germans, who were already being pounded by the service's B-17 Flying Fortress and Consolidated B-24 Liberator bombers, but rather in Asia against the Japanese who were all but immune to American air attack. The first unit to operate the Superfortress was the 58th Very Heavy Bombardment Wing, which had been activated in June 1943 before the delivery of its first YB-29 aircraft, and the arrival of these aircraft during July allowed the unit to familiarise itself with the intricacies of the new bomber. The first B-29s were delivered by Boeing in the autumn of 1943, and aircraft from the Bell and Martin production lines started to reach operational units in 1944: B-29 deliveries amounted to 2,181 aircraft in the form of 1,620 from Boeing, 357 from Bell and 204 from Martin.

The 40th, 444th, 462nd and 468th Very Heavy

The considerable weight of the Boeing B-29 Superfortress, especially at take-off, resulted in the adoption of two-wheel main landing gear units that retracted fully into the underside of the inboard engine nacelles after take-off.

Bombardment Groups of the 58th Very Heavy Bombardment Wing reached India in the spring of 1944, and their first operational mission in June of that year – via staging airfields in China – was to attack Japanese targets in Bangkok. The raids were soon extended in scope and range, including the Japanese home islands from the second mission, but it was soon clear that the simple forward bases of the US 20th Army Air Force's XX Bomber Command in China were too distant from Japan and from their rear bases in India for the B-29s to fight an effective campaign: much of the Command's B-29 strength was required to ferry fuel, munitions and supplies to China, leaving only a very modest number of aircraft to wage the war against Japan, and then only with indifferent results. This was one of the primary reasons for the US campaign to capture the Mariana Islands (Saipan, Tinian and Guam), and American engineers soon created five air bases each large enough to accommodate a complete 180-bomber wing of XXI Bomber Command.

The first raid against Tokyo was flown from the Marianas in November 1944, but results were still disappointing. The raids were flown by day at high altitude with modest loads of HE bombs, and it was only in February 1945 that a new commander realised that the wrong tactics were being used. Major General Curtis E. LeMay therefore switched the B-29s to nocturnal medium- and low-altitude raids with a large proportion of incendiary bombs: as the Japanese lacked an effective night-fighter arm, night raids allowed all but the tail armament to be removed, making it possible to carry a larger disposable warload; and low- and medium-altitude release improved bombing accuracy as there were no jetstream winds to disturb the bombs' trajectories, and incendiaries proved far more devastating than HE bombs for the destruction of Japan's cities. Some of the aircraft were further modified with the APQ-7 radar bomb sight using an antenna that was carried in a 14ft (4.27m) 'wing' carried under the fuselage. XX Bomber Command was then relocated to the Mariana Islands, and from the five bases on these three 'unsinkable aircraft carriers' the B-29s of XX and XXI Bomber Commands burned the heart out of Japan while also dropping HE bombs to destroy railroads and munitions factories.

To all intents and purposes, therefore, the war against Japan had been won before the dropping of the two A-bombs on Hiroshima and Nagasaki, but these two cataclysmic events were required to convince the Japanese that this really was the case.

B-29A Superfortress: These 1,119 aircraft were delivered from the Boeing-run facility at Renton, and were completed to a standard that differed from that of the B-29 in its powerplant of four R-3350-57/59 radial piston engines, incorporation of the four-gun forward dorsal barbette, and adoption of a new wing structure that increased span to 142ft 2.75in (43.35m). Whereas the wing of the B-29 had been based on a two-part centre section bolted together on the centreline and installed in the fuselage as a single unit carrying all four engine nacelles, that of the B-29A was based on a shorter-span centre section that projected only slightly from the fuselage sides and carried two intermediate sections, each carrying two engine nacelles, to which were attached the standard outer sections.

Other details of the B-29A included a length of 99ft 0in (30.175m); height of 29ft 7in (9.02m); empty and maximum take-off weights of 71,360 and 141,100lb (32,369 and 64,003kg) respectively; maximum level speed of 311kt (358mph; 576km/h) at 25,000ft (7,620m); cruising speed of 200kt (230mph; 370km/h) at optimum altitude; typical range of 3,561nm (4,100 miles; 6,598km); climb to 20,000ft (6,096m) in 38min 0sec, and service ceiling of 31,850ft (9,708m).

A number of the aircraft were later converted to TB-29A Superfortress crew trainer standard, and one of these machines was further converted as the sole ETB-29A Superfortress for experimental parasite fighter trials, with one Republic F-84B Thunderjet fighter flexibly attached at each wingtip for towed carriage until released in combat.

B-29B Superfortress: Production of the B-29 series was completed by this variant, of which 311 were delivered by Bell with defensive armament limited to the tail guns, which were laid and fired automatically with the aid of the APG-15B radar system. Other details of the B-29A included a span of 141ft 2.75in (43.05m) with an area of 1,736.00sq ft (161.27sq m); length of 99ft 0in (30.175m); height of 29ft 7in (9.02m); empty and maximum take-off weights of 69,000 and 137,500lb (31,298 and 62,370kg) respectively; maximum level speed of 316kt (364mph; 586km/h) at 25,000ft (7,620m); cruising speed of 198kt (228mph; 367km/h) at optimum altitude; typical range of 3,647nm (4,200 miles; 6,759km); climb to 20,000ft (6,096m) in 38min 0sec, and service ceiling of 32,000ft (9,753m).

Production of an additional 5,092 bombers of the B-29 series was terminated with the end of World War II, and the last of 3,627 aircraft (including prototypes and service test machines) was delivered in June 1946. Other designations in the B-29 alphanumeric sequence that were not taken up or were used only for experimental developments were EB-29B (one B-29B converted as motherplane for the experimental air-launched McDonnell Douglas XF-85 Goblin fighter); B-29C (one B-29 that was to have been tested with improved R-3350 engines); B-29D (an improved Model 345-2 made of 75ST aluminium alloy and powered by four Pratt & Whitney R-4360 radial engines for post-war construction as the B-50 series); and XB-29E (one conversion for fire-control system testing).

B-29F Superfortress: This designation was allocated to six examples of the B-29 that undertook cold-weather tests in Alaska and were then converted back to basic B-29 standard. Other projects or prototype conversions included the XB-29G (one B-29 converted with an underfuselage pantograph for flight testing of General Electric turbojets), and the XB-29H (one B-29A conversion for special weapons tests).

Consolidated Model 32 (B-24 Liberator)

Manufacturer: Consolidated (later Consolidated-Vultee) Aircraft Corporation

Country of origin: USA

Specification: B-24J Liberator

Type: Heavy bomber

Accommodation: Pilot and co-pilot side by side on the enclosed flightdeck, and bombardier, navigator, radio operator and five gunners carried in the fuselage

Entered service: 1941

Left service: 1967

Armament (fixed): Two 0.5in (12.7mm) Browning trainable forward-firing machine-guns in the power-operated Motor Products (Consolidated) nose turret, two

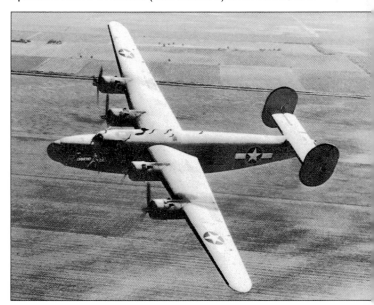

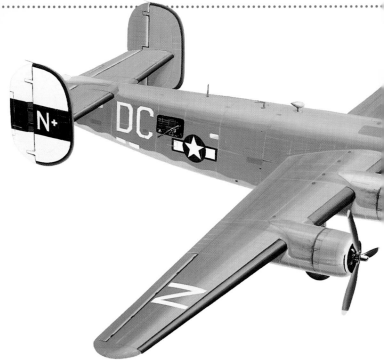

0.5in (12.7mm) Browning trainable machine-guns in the power-operated Martin dorsal turret, two 0.5in (12.7mm) Browning trainable machine-guns in the power-operated Briggs-Sperry ventral turret, two 0.5in (12.7mm) Browning trainable rearward-firing machine-guns in the power-operated Motor Products (Consolidated) tail turret, and two 0.5in (12.7mm) Browning trainable lateral-firing machine-guns in two beam positions

Armament (disposable): Up to 12,000lb (5,443kg) of disposable stores carried in two weapons bays side by side in the lower fuselage with each bay rated at 4,000lb (1,814kg) and on two underwing racks each rated at 4,000lb (1,814kg), and generally comprising two 4,000lb (1,814kg) bombs, or four 2,000lb (907kg) bombs, or eight 1,000lb (454kg) bombs or sixteen 500lb (227kg) bombs carried internally, and bombs of up to 4,000lb (1,814kg) weight carried under the wings

Operational equipment: Standard communication and navigation equipment, plus a Norden optical bomb sight and optical gunsights

With its clean design and high-aspect-ratio wing, the Consolidated B-24 Liberator had very good range, while its capacious fuselage allowed the type to carry a substantial warload and also made it feasible to adapt the type for several other roles. As a result, the Liberator was built in larger numbers than any other American warplane of World War II despite the fact that it was a four-engined type.

Powerplant: Four Pratt & Whitney R-1830-65 radial piston engines each rated at 1,200hp (895kW) for take-off and 1,050hp (783kW) at 7,500ft (2,286m)

Fuel capacity: Internal fuel 1,968.5 Imp gal (8,947 litres) plus provision for 1,040.9 Imp gal (4,731.75 litres) of auxiliary fuel in 374.7 Imp gal (1,703.4 litres) auxiliary wing tankage and 666.2 Imp gal (3,028.3 litres) auxiliary weapons-bay tankage; external fuel none

Dimensions: Span 110ft 0in (33.53m); aspect ratio 11.55; area 1,048.00sq ft (97.36sq m); length 67ft 2in (20.47m); height 18ft 0in (5.49m); wheel track 25ft 7.5in (7.81m); wheelbase 16ft 0in (4.88m)

Weights: Empty 36,500lb (16,556kg) equipped; normal take-off 56,000lb (25,401kg); maximum take-off 65,000lb (29,484kg)

Performance: Maximum level speed 'clean' 260.5kt (300mph; 483km/h) at 30,000ft (9,145m); cruising speed 187kt (215mph; 346km/h) at optimum altitude; maximum range 2,866nm (3,300 miles; 5,310km); typical range 1,824nm (2,100 miles; 3,380km) with a weapons load of 5,000lb (2,268kg); climb to 20,000ft (6,096m) in 25min 0sec; service ceiling 30,000ft (9,145m)

Variants

B-24A Liberator: Produced in many variants for both operational and training tasks, the Liberator was built in larger numbers (18,431 machines in total) than any other warplane of American design during World War II and was delivered in greater quantities than any other bomber in aviation history. These would be remarkable facts in their own right, but are of particular note for the fact that the Liberator was a four-engined machine.

The origins of the type can be traced to January 1939 when Reuben H. Fleet and Isaac M. 'Mac' Laddon, respectively chairman and chief designer of the Consolidated Aircraft Corporation, approached the USAAC with an offer to design and build a bomber superior to the Boeing B-17. The corporation felt that it was able to offer a machine superior to the Boeing bomber after being approached by the USAAC to become a second source for B-17 production, and Consolidated engineers who had travelled from San Diego in California to the Boeing facility at Seattle in Washington returned with the suggestion that an improved aeroplane could be designed on the basis of the high-aspect-ratio wing evolved by Laddon, (and on the basis of the concept patented by David R. Davis), for the Model 28 flying boat that had entered production as the PBY for the US Navy.

The USAAC was impressed with the Consolidated proposal and inspected a Consolidated mock-up in January 1939. The service then issued a competitive requirement to Martin and Sikorsky, but this was nothing more than a formality as it gave these two 'contenders' a mere three weeks to create their proposals. In February 1939 the Consolidated Model 32 design was approved, and in March a single XB-24 prototype was ordered for delivery by the end of the year, later orders adding seven YB-24 service test aircraft and 38 B-24A initial production bombers.

Consolidated made rapid progress with the completion of the detail design and the construction of the prototype, which emerged for its first flight in December 1939 as a large shoulder-wing monoplane of all-metal construction with fabric-covered control surfaces, a rectangular-section fuselage whose corners were rounded for reduced drag, a high-set tail unit whose horizontal surface carried endplate vertical surfaces, a high-aspect-ratio wing that carried outboard ailerons and inboard Fowler flaps, and tricycle landing gear. This last feature was of the fully retractable

a ventral tray carrying four or six 20mm fixed forward-firing cannon to provide a significant punch in the war against the German U-boats that had previously been able to operate on the surface in the mid-Atlantic region.

The USAAC received the last YB-24, fitted with self-sealing fuel tanks and protective armour for the crew, during May 1941 and then the final nine B-24A aircraft in the middle of the same year. The B-24A had a wing identical to that of all other B-24 variants, but differed in details such as its powerplant of four R-1830-33 radial engines each rated at 1,200hp (895kW) at optimum altitude; defensive armament of six 0.5in (12.7mm) and two 0.3in (7.62mm) Browning trainable machine-guns; offensive armament of 4,000lb (1,814kg); length of 63ft 9in (19.43m); height of 18ft 8in (5.69m); empty weight of 30,000lb (13,608kg); maximum take-off weight of 53,600lb (24,313kg); maximum level speed of 254kt (292mph; 470km/h) at 15,000ft (4,572m); cruising speed of 198kt (228mph; 367km/h) at optimum altitude; range of 1,911nm (2,200 miles; 3,540km); climb to 10,000ft (3,048m) in 5min 36sec, and service ceiling of 30,500ft (9,296m).

LB-30 Liberator: Delivered to the RAF for service as the Liberator Mk II, this variant had an additional nose section that increased overall length by 2ft 7in (0.79m) to 66ft 4in (20.22m), power-operated dorsal and tail turrets increasing the defensive armament to fourteen 0.303in (7.7mm) Browning trainable machine-guns including four each in the power-operated Boulton Paul dorsal and tail turrets, and a powerplant of four commercial rather than military R-1830-S3C4-G Twin Wasp radial engines each rated at 1,200hp (895kW) at optimum altitude and driving a three-blade Curtiss Electric metal propeller of the constant-speed type rather than the comparable Hamilton Standard Hydromatic propeller that was standard on all other Liberator variants.

Production totalled 139 aircraft, all intended for RAF squadrons operating in the Middle East. As deliveries were being made, however, the United States was drawn into World War II by the Japanese attack on Pearl Harbor and the Philippines during December 1941, and 75 aircraft were repossessed for service with the USAAF. It was aircraft of this variant that made the first American bombing mission with the type when machines of the 7th Bomb Group operated from an airfield in Java against Japanese forces invading the Netherlands East Indies. Others of the aircraft were deployed to Alaska, Hawaii and the Panama Canal Zone for long-range ocean patrol bomber use, and 24 of the aircraft finally reached the British, who thus received a total of 88 such aircraft.

B-24C Liberator: These nine aircraft were delivered from December 1941 to the USAAF with R-1830-41 radial engines each rated at 1,200hp (895kW) at optimum altitude, self-sealing fuel tanks, and three power-operated turrets in the nose, dorsal and tail positions.

B-24D Liberator: This was the first variant to enter large-scale production, some 2,728 aircraft coming from the Consolidated line and a further 10 from the Douglas line. The delivery of aircraft from Douglas is evidence of the importance that was attached to the Liberator by the USAAF: Consolidated had built two new production facilities at Lindbergh Field in San Diego and at Fort Worth in Texas, and the efforts of these two centres was increasingly supplemented by the Douglas facility at Tulsa in Oklahoma, by Ford at Willow Run in Michigan (where components were also produced for other production centres), and by North American at Dallas in Texas.

Delivered from January 1942, the B-24D had a powerplant of four R-1830-43 or -65 radial engines each rated at 1,200hp (895kW) at optimum altitude and supplied with fuel from an internal capacity increased from 1,968.5 Imp gal/8,948.7 litres (in early aircraft with a maximum take-off weight of 55,000lb/24,948kg and a defensive armament of seven machine-guns) to a maximum of 3,009.3 Imp gal/13,680.4 litres (in later aircraft with a maximum take-off weight of 64,000lb/29,030kg and a defensive armament of 10 machine-guns).

Of these aircraft, 272 were completed with a ventral turret (a Bendix unit in 179 aircraft and a Sperry unit in the other 93 aircraft) that increased the variant's defensive armament from seven or eight to ten 0.5in (12.7mm) Browning trainable machine-guns; the offensive load was also increased to a maximum of 8,800lb (3,992kg) in the form of eight 1,100lb (499kg) bombs. The other primary details of the late-production B-24D, where different from the B-24J, included a length of 66ft 4in (20.22m); height of 17ft 11in (5.46m); empty and normal take-off weights of 32,605 and 60,000lb (14,790 and 27,216kg), maximum level speed of 263kt (303mph; 488km/h) at 25,000ft (7,620m);

cruising speed of 174kt (200mph; 322km/h) at optimum altitude; maximum range of 3,040nm (3,500 miles; 5,633km); typical range of 1,997nm (2,300 miles; 3,701km) with a weapons load of 5,000lb (2,268kg); climb to 20,000ft (6,096m) in 22min 0sec, and service ceiling of 32,000ft (9,753m).

Ten aircraft adapted for the night bomber role with a radar bomb sight received the revised designation SB-24D Liberator and were used with some success against Japanese targets.

B-24E Liberator: This was a development of the B-24D with different propeller blades, and production amounted to 801 aircraft: delivered from September 1942, the 167 Douglas-built aircraft had a powerplant of four R-1830-43 radial engines, while the 634 Ford-built aircraft had a powerplant of four R-1830-65 radial engines. The type was delayed in production, primarily by the conflict between Ford's vehicle and aircraft interests, and was obsolescent even as it entered service. The type was therefore used mostly for training within the continental USA, and some 160 of them were adapted with a General Electric fire-control system as gunnery trainers for the Boeing B-29 Superfortress programme.

The sole XB-24F was a B-24D conversion for evaluation of a thermal de-icing system.

B-24G Liberator: These 430 North American-built aircraft were similar to the B-24D with the R-1830-43 radial engine but with provision for a power-operated Emerson nose turret, carrying two 0.5in (12.7mm) Browning trainable forward-firing machine-guns, in an effort to counter the type of head-on attack that German and Japanese fighters had found to be the most successful tactic against the early Liberators. Early aircraft had no ventral turret, but a Briggs-Sperry ball turret was reintroduced later in the production run at the same time as the powerplant was revised to four R-1830-65 radial engines.

B-24H Liberator: Built by Consolidated, Douglas and Ford, this model was introduced in June 1943 as a type similar to the late-production B-24G and therefore was equipped with an Emerson nose turret and the retractable Sperry ventral ball turret that had been introduced on some later B-24D bombers. The first B-24H bombers had

With each bomber possessing nose, tail, dorsal, ventral and lateral defensive machine guns, close formations of Consolidated B-24 Liberators were well able to put up a formidable weight of heavy machine gun fire to deter the efforts of attacking fighters. These are B-24J bombers of the US 15th Air Force during an attack on the oil installations at Ploesti in Romania during May 1944.

a powerplant of four R-1830-43 radial engines that were replaced by a quartet of R-1830-65 radial engines in later machines, which also had superior beam positions with fairings that improved the airflow and also made life more comfortable for the two waist gunners. The total of 3,100 B-24H models was delivered from Fort Worth (738 machines), Tulsa (582 machines) and Willow Run (1,780 machines).

B-24J Liberator: With a total of 6,678 delivered from all five factories in the Liberator production group, this was the most extensively built variant of the whole series, and was in essence an improved B-24H with hydraulically operated Consolidated-designed but Motor Products-built nose and tail turrets, a Martin dorsal turret, a Briggs-Sperry ventral turret, a new C-1 autopilot, a new M-series bomb sight, and other equipment changes including electronic turbocharger regulators.

A number of the aircraft were later converted as crew trainers with the revised designation TB-24J Liberator.

B-24L Liberator: Delivered to the extent of 1,667 aircraft (1,250 from Willow Run and 417 from Lindbergh Field), this was a development of the B-24J with a new lightweight tail position designed by Consolidated, with two manually operated 0.5in (12.7mm) Browning trainable rearward-firing machine-guns.

A number of the aircraft were later converted as RB-24L Liberator crew trainers for the Boeing B-29 Super-fortress programme, with square-cut nose transparencies and remotely controlled barbettes in the chin, dorsal, ventral and tail positions; some of these aircraft were later modified as TB-24L Liberator radar operator trainers.

Handley Page H.P.57 Halifax

Manufacturer: Handley Page Ltd.

Country of origin: UK

Specification: Halifax B.Mk III

Type: Heavy bomber

Accommodation: Pilot and co-pilot side by side on the enclosed flightdeck, and navigator/bombardier/gunner, radio operator, flight engineer and two gunners carried in the fuselage

Entered service: November 1940

Left service: March 1952

Armament (fixed): One 0.303in (7.7mm) Vickers 'K' trainable forward-firing machine-gun with 300 rounds in the nose position, four 0.303in (7.7mm) Browning trainable machine-guns with 1,160 rounds per gun in the power-operated Boulton Paul Type A Mk III dorsal turret, and four 0.303in (7.7mm) Browning trainable machine-guns with 1,160 rounds per gun in the power-operated Boulton Paul Type E tail turret

Armament (disposable): Up to 14,500lb (6,577kg) of disposable stores carried in a lower-fuselage weapons bay rated at 13,000lb (5,897kg) and in six wing cells each rated at 500lb (227kg), and generally comprising one 8,000lb (3,629kg) bomb, or two 4,000lb (1,814kg) bombs, or four 2,000lb (907kg) bombs, or two 2,000lb (907kg) and six 1,000lb (454kg) bombs, or eight 1,000lb (454kg) bombs, or two 1,500lb (680kg) mines and six 500lb (227kg) bombs, or nine 500lb (227kg) bombs carried in the weapons bay, and six 500 or 250lb (227 or 113kg) bombs carried in the wing cells

Operational equipment: Standard communication and navigation equipment, plus an optical bomb sight, optical gunsights and H2S nav/attack radar

Powerplant: Four Bristol Hercules XVI radial piston

engines each rated at 1,615hp (1,204kW) for take-off and 1,455hp (1,085kW) at 12,000ft (3,658m)

Fuel capacity: Internal fuel 1,998 Imp gal (9,082.9 litres) plus provision for up to 576 Imp gal (2,618.5 litres) of auxiliary fuel in six wing weapon-cell tanks; external fuel none

Dimensions: Span 98ft 10in (30.12m); aspect ratio 7.81; area 1,250.00sq ft (116.125sq m); length 71ft 7in (21.82m); height 20ft 9in (6.32m)

Weights: Empty 38,240lb (17,346kg) equipped; maximum take-off 65,000lb (29,484kg)

Performance: Maximum level speed 'clean' 245kt (282mph; 454km/h) at 13,500ft (4,115m) declining to 241kt (278mph; 447km/h) at 6,000ft (1,829m); cruising speed, economical 187kt (215mph; 346km/h) at 20,000ft (6,096m); typical range 1,724nm (1,985 miles; 3,194km) with a 7,000lb (3,175kg) weapons load declining to 894.5nm (1,030 miles; 1,658km) with a 13,000lb (5,897kg) weapons load; maximum rate of climb at sea level 960ft (293m) per minute; climb to 20,000ft (6,096m) in 37min 30sec; service ceiling 24,000ft (7,315m)

Variants
Halifax Mk I: Although overshadowed by the superb Avro Lancaster, which it partnered throughout much of World War II in the great night bombing offensive undertaken by the RAF's Bomber Command against German urban and

Although second in importance to the Avro Lancaster in the British heavy night bombing effort during World War II, the Handley Page Halifax was nonetheless a very worthy bomber in its own right. This is a machine of No.78 Squadron of RAF Bomber Command.

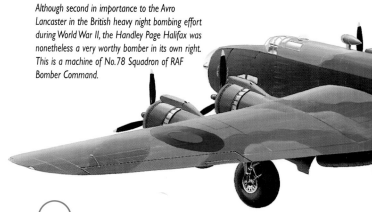

industrial regions, the Halifax was still a magnificent warplane that deserves greater attention than it has generally received. The early Halifax bombers were not quite as 'right' as the early Lancaster warplanes, and it took considerable effort and time to eliminate all its initial problems. The Halifax then matured as an exceptional bomber that in its late-war variants was faster than the Lancaster, and could carry an equivalent weapons load even though it was not as fuel economical and lacked the Lancaster's rate of climb and agility.

The origins of the Halifax can be traced to the Air Ministry's B.1/35 requirement for a twin-engined bomber to succeed the Vickers Wellington. The Handley Page design team, under the supervision of George Volkert, planned the H.P.55 as a mid-wing type with a powerplant of two Bristol Hercules radial or Rolls-Royce Merlin inverted-Vee piston engines, and the Air Ministry ordered a single prototype in October 1935. Then followed the P.13/36 requirement for a faster medium bomber, and the company decided to recast the H.P.55 as the H.P.56 with the wing reduced in span from 95ft 0in (28.96m) to 90ft 0in (27.43m) and carrying the twin-engined powerplant. The company suggested to the Air Ministry that the development of the H.P.56 should be undertaken in two stages, the first with a powerplant of two Hercules radial engines and the second with the considerably more potent arrangement of two Rolls-Royce Vulture X-type piston engines. Given the pace and scope of the German rearmament programme, however, the Air Ministry wanted to proceed as rapidly as possible and, in April 1937, placed a contract for two H.P.56 prototypes each with a powerplant of two Vulture engines.

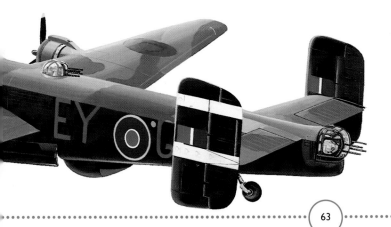

The type was schemed with an essentially all-metal structure based on a rectangular-section fuselage with rounded corners: this was to carry a high-set tail unit with endplate vertical surfaces at the tips of the horizontal surface, and a cantilever mid-set wing with a flat centre section of the constant-chord type and dihedraled outer panels that were tapered in thickness and chord; the trailing edges carried outboard ailerons and inboard slotted flaps. The airframe was to be completed by the tailwheel landing gear, which included a tail unit that retracted into the underside of the rear fuselage, and main units that retracted into the underside of the two wing-mounted engine nacelles; the defensive armament was to comprise two 0.303in (7.7mm) Browning trainable forward-firing machine-guns in a power-operated Boulton Paul nose turret, four 0.303in (7.7mm) Browning trainable rearward-firing machine-guns in a power-operated Boulton Paul tail turret, and two 0.303in (7.7mm) Vickers 'K' trainable lateral-firing machine-guns in two manually operated beam positions.

In theory this H.P.56 package offered the promise of an excellent warplane, but in practice Handley Page became increasingly concerned about the Vulture engine, which was proving very troublesome in development. The company therefore approached the Air Ministry with the suggestion that the H.P.56 be revised as the H.P.57 with a longer-span wing carrying a powerplant of four Merlin engines. The Air Ministry gave its approval for the change in September 1937, and the H.P.57 began to take shape with a wing enlarged in span to 98ft 10in (30.12m) and including outer panels that still carried large Handley Page automatic leading-edge slats, but which were tapered on both the leading and trailing edges rather than on just the leading edge as with the H.P.56.

Work on the completion of the first type was advanced as rapidly as possible, and this made its maiden flight in October 1939 (less than two months after the outbreak of World War II) with a powerplant of four Merlin IX engines each driving a three-blade propeller of the constant-speed type, but with no armament. The second prototype followed in August 1940 with the same powerplant driving different Rotol propellers with densified wood blades, and this machine had full armament but no leading-edge slats.

Production was already under way by this time, the Air Ministry having ordered the H.P.57 into production late in 1938 and allocating the name 'Halifax' early in 1939.

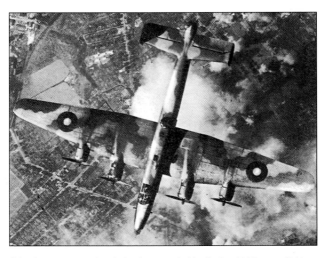

Although no quite as good as the Avro Lancaster, the Handley Page Halifax was a highly capable and versatile warplane, especially in its later versions with the Bristol Hercules radial engine.

Production on a very large scale was envisaged, with initial aircraft coming from the English Electric line that was currently delivering the Handley Page Hampden medium bomber, and then being supplemented by deliveries from an industrial grouping that eventually included the Rootes Group, the Fairey Aviation Co. Ltd. and the London Aircraft Production Group. The Halifax Mk I entered service in November 1940 as the industrial machine began to gather production pace, and the first of an eventual 36 RAF Bomber Command squadrons to receive the type was No. 35 Squadron, which flew its first mission in March 1941.

The type was fully appreciated from the beginning, but as larger numbers of aircraft reached first-line squadrons, problems became apparent with the main landing gear unit retraction system and the reduction gears of the Merlin X engine, rated at 1,280hp (954kW). The cause of the former problem was traced to faulty uplocks and a leaking hydraulic system, and was gradually cured by design changes and the locking of the tailwheel unit in the extended position, while the cause of the latter problem was eventually traced to aerodynamically induced vibration that was mitigated although not cured by the replacement of the original three-blade propellers by four-blade units. There was a shortage of such propellers, however, and aircraft were often seen with three-blade propellers on their inboard engines and four-blade units on their outboard engines, or even with a single four-blade propeller on the port outboard engine.

Deliveries of the Halifax Mk I totalled 84 aircraft in three subvariants: the Halifax Mk I Series 1 had a powerplant of four Merlin X engines and was stressed for a maximum take-off weight of 58,000lb (26,309kg); the Halifax Mk I Series 2 had a powerplant of four Merlin X engines and was stressed for a maximum take-off weight of 60,000lb (27,216kg); and the Halifax Mk I Series 3 had a powerplant of four Merlin X or Merlin XX engines and increased fuel capacity. The Halifax Mk I had the armament of the H.P.56 and the wing of the Halifax Mk III, but otherwise differed in details such as its length of 70ft 1in (21.36m); maximum level speed of 230kt (265mph; 426km/h) at 17,500ft (5,334m); range of 1,094nm (1,260 miles; 2,028km) with maximum weapons load, increasing to 2,084nm (2,400 miles; 3,862km) with reduced weapons load; initial climb rate of 750ft (229m) per minute, and service ceiling of 22,800ft (6,949m).

Halifax Mk II: Built to the extent of 1,977 aircraft that received the revised designation Halifax B.Mk II in 1942, this was the first large-scale production model and was in essence a development of the Halifax Mk I Series 3, with a powerplant of four Merlin XX or Merlin 22 engines each rated at 1,390hp (1,036kW) and fitted with an improved supercharger. The initial production model was the Halifax B.Mk II Series 1 that had a powerplant of four Merlin XXS engines and also introduced a power-operated Boulton Paul dorsal turret armed with two 0.303in (7.7mm) Browning trainable machine-guns.

Despite the extra power offered by the uprated powerplant, the weight and drag of the new turret seriously affected performance. The decision that performance was of greater importance led to the Halifax B.Mk II Series 1 (Special) that omitted both the new dorsal turret and also the original nose turret; most of the aircraft were also stripped of their flame-damper exhausts as crews felt that the 17.5kt (20mph; 32km/h) additional cruising speed and higher ceiling were more useful than the damping of exhaust flames that were only visible within a range of a few hundred feet. These changes considerably improved performance, and this was further boosted by the adoption of Merlin 22 engines each rated at 1,390hp (1,036kW) in the Halifax B.Mk II Series 1A that reintroduced a power-

The Handley Page Halifax Mk I has Rolls-Royce Merlin Vee engines and no dorsal turret, while the Halifax Mk II introduced a dorsal turret.

operated dorsal turret in the form of a low-drag Boulton Paul unit with four 0.303in (7.7mm) Browning trainable machine-guns, and also featured a moulded Perspex nose fairing fitted with one 0.303in (7.7mm) Browning or Vickers 'K' trainable forward-firing machine-gun. This increased the overall length to 71ft 7in (21.82m) but improved the line of the forward fuselage and thereby increased speed.

A number of Halifax B.Mk II Series IA bombers were later converted as Halifax GR.Mk II Series IA aircraft with specialised equipment and the nose-mounted 0.303in (7.7mm) machine-gun replaced by a 0.5in (12.7mm) Browning weapon for improved firepower against the anti-aircraft gunners of surfaced U-boats.

Halifax B.Mk III: The main limitations suffered by early Halifax bombers were a lack of speed, climb and service ceiling, which resulted from the early bombers' restriction to relatively low-powered versions of the Merlin engine, whose high-powered versions were required for high-performance types such as the Bristol Beaufighter attack fighter, de Havilland Mosquito multi-role warplane and Supermarine Spitfire fighter. In October 1942, however, Handley Page revised a Halifax B.Mk II 'hack' with a powerplant of four Bristol Hercules radial piston engines as the prototype of the radial-engined H.P.61 series: as a result, performance was generally improved in every regard except range (the 2,320cu in/38 litre radial engine burned more fuel than the 1,650cu in/27 litre Vee engine), and the type's handling characteristics were enhanced.

The success of this re-engining led to the introduction of the Halifax B.Mk III production model, of which the first flew in July 1943 with a powerplant of four Hercules XVI engines, each rated at 1,615hp (1,204kW) and driving a three-blade de Havilland metal propeller of the constant-speed type and installed without a spinner but with long flame-damper exhausts. Other changes were an effective actuation system for the tailwheel; revised quadrilateral endplate vertical surfaces on the tail unit; a wing increased in span to 104ft 2in (31.75m) with an area of 1,275.00sq ft (118.45sq m); provision for H2S nav/attack radar; and provision for ventral protection in the form of a blister position carrying one 0.5in (12.7mm) Browning trainable rearward-firing machine-gun.

The Halifax B.Mk III was a marked improvement over the previous models, and in this form the type was now allowed to operate against targets that had hitherto been regarded as too difficult for the Halifax. Production of the Halifax B.Mk III totalled 2,091 aircraft, and the rapidly accelerating availability of this model allowed the removal of all Merlin-engined models from operations over Germany.

Halifax B.Mk V: The Halifax B.Mk IV was a model that was projected but not built except as a prototype conversion with modified engine mountings, so the next variant to enter production was the Halifax B.Mk V that was a development of the Halifax B.Mk II with the original Messier landing gear units and hydraulic system replaced by Dowty units. Most of the aircraft were fitted with four-blade propellers, and production totalled 904 aircraft from Fairey and Rootes.

The type was built in Halifax B.Mk V Series I, B.Mk V Series I (Special) and B.Mk V Series IA subvariants.

Halifax B.Mk VI: First flown in October 1944 and built to the extent of 557 aircraft delivered by Handley Page and English Electric, this was an improved version of the Halifax B.Mk IV intended for operations against the Japanese in South-East Asia, and fitted with Hercules 100 radial engines each rated at 1,800hp (1,342kW), fuel-injection carburettors with filters, and a revised fuel system that was enlarged and pressurised.

Halifax B.Mk VII: With production of the Hercules 100 radial engine lagging behind that of the Halifax B.Mk VI airframe, a final 193 aircraft were completed to this standard with Hercules XVI radial engines, and these machines were used by French and Polish squadrons.

Variants

He 111H-1: The He 111H was Germany's most important medium bomber of World War II, and was derived from the pre-war He 111P. The two variants shared a common airframe (differing from their predecessors mainly in their revised and fully glazed forward fuselage with an unstepped cockpit, and a ventral gondola), but differed in their powerplant: the He 111P was designed for the Daimler-Benz DB 601 inverted-Vee piston engine while the He 111H was planned with the Junkers Jumo 211 inverted-Vee piston engine.

The prototype for the He 111H series was the He 111 V19 that first flew in January 1939, and this was followed from May of the same year by the He 111A-0 pre-production and He 111H-1 initial production models that were identical to the He 111P-2 in all but their powerplant of two Jumo 211A-1 engines each rated at 1,010hp (753kW) for take-off and 960hp (716kW) at 4,920ft (1,500m); the defensive armament of the He 111H-1 was three 0.312in (7.92mm) MG 15 trainable machine-guns located singly in the manually operated nose, dorsal and ventral positions. The Luftwaffe placed great importance on this improved bomber model, as may be gauged from the fact that Heinkel and its licensees delivered some 400 of the type in the four months preceding the outbreak of World War II in September 1939: the He 111H therefore represented about half of the Luftwaffe's He 111 force at the start of hostilities.

He 111H-2: Introduced just as World War II was starting, this was an improved version of the He 111H-1, with a powerplant of two Jumo 211A-3 engines each rated at 1,100hp (820kW) for take-off and, soon after the start of the production run, with the defensive armament doubled to six 0.312in (7.92mm) MG 15 trainable machine-guns.

He 111H-3: Introduced in November 1939, this was a development of the He 111H-2 for the bombing and anti-ship roles, with a powerplant of two Jumo 211D-1 engines each rated at 1,200hp (895kW) for take-off and with the gun armament bolstered by one 20mm MG FF trainable forward-firing cannon in the ventral gondola. The disposable armament comprised 4,409lb (2,000kg) of bombs carried internally, and the weapons bay could alternatively be fitted with an auxiliary fuel tank. A number of the aircraft were also supplied to the Romanian air force, which was so impressed with the type that arrangements were made for it to be built under license in Romania by the Fabrica de Avione SET, deliveries beginning in 1942.

He 111H-4: Deliveries of the He 111H-3 continued throughout 1940, and were complemented during the year by the arrival of the He 111H-4. This was a development of the He 111H-3, initially with the same powerplant but later with two Jumo 211F-1 engines each rated at 1,400hp (1,044kW) for take-off and 1,200hp (895kW) at 16,405ft (5,000m), and with a revised disposable armament capability. The port side of the weapons bay was blanked off and strengthened for the external carriage of two 2,205lb (1,000kg) SC/PD1000 bombs or one 3,968lb (1,800kg) SC/PD1800 bomb.

He 111H-5: This was a variant of the He 111H-4 with a powerplant of two Jumo 211D-1 engines, provision for both halves of the weapons bay to carry an auxiliary fuel tank, and with the disposable armament limited to 5,511lb (2,500kg) of weapons carried on two external hardpoints at a maximum take-off weight of 30,985lb (14,055kg).

He 111H-6: Both the He 111H-4 and He 111H-5 lasted in production long enough for a number of improvements to be added in stages, and all these improvements were incorporated as standard in the He 111H-6 that entered production late in 1941. The He 111H-6 had a powerplant of two Jumo 211F-1 engines, a gun armament of one 20mm MG FF cannon and six 0.312in (7.92mm) MG 15 machine-guns, in some aircraft a remotely controlled 0.312in (7.92mm) MG 17 fixed rearward-firing machine-gun in the tailcone to deter stern attackers, and provision for the externally carried disposable load to include two 1,686lb (765kg) LT F5b air-launched torpedoes under the fuselage. The He 111H-6 very quickly became the most extensively used version of the He 111H series, for it was a delight to handle even at maximum take-off weight, was stable yet manoeuvrable, possessed adequate performance and defensive firepower, and was extremely versatile.

It had been planned to phase the type out of production during 1942 in favour of the Heinkel He 177A Greif heavy bomber and the Junkers Ju 288 medium bomber, but the failure of both these types meant that production of the He 111H-6 was maintained.

He 111H-7: This was a variant of the He 111H-6 with minor equipment changes.

He 111H-8: This was a development of the He 111H-6, produced to the extent of 30 aircraft converted from He 111H-3 and He 111H-5 standards with a balloon cable fender/cutter arrangement extending from a point ahead of the nose to both wingtips. This weighed some 551lb (250kg) and required the addition of ballast in the tail to preserve the centre of gravity in the right position, and the extra weight so affected performance and weapons load that the aircraft saw only limited operational service before being relegated to use as glider tugs with the revised designation He 111H-8/R2.

He 111H-9: This was a variant of the He 111H-6 with minor equipment changes.

He 111H-10: This was a development of the He 111H-6 with a powerplant of two Jumo 211F-2 engines, balloon cable cutting devices in the wing leading edges, and the positions of the forward-firing 0.312in (7.92mm) machine-gun and 20mm cannon reversed so that the MG FF cannon was installed in the nose and the MG 15 machine-gun in the ventral gondola.

He 111H-11: This was a development of the He 111H-10 with improvements to crew protection and defensive armament. The dorsal position was fully enclosed with screens of toughened glass, and was provided with a 0.51in (13mm) MG 131 trainable rearward-firing machine-gun in place of the original 0.312in (7.92mm) MG 15 weapon; the ventral defence was boosted by the replacement of the single 0.312in (7.92mm) MG 15 machine-gun by two 0.312in (7.92mm) MG 81 weapons; and jettisonable armour plates were added over particularly vulnerable areas. Provision was also made for an improved offensive capability by the development of a carrier plate that could be added under the fuselage for five 551lb (250kg) SC250 bombs.

The He 111H-11 proved successful within the limits of the basic airframe's increasing obsolescence, and the type's steadily worsening vulnerability was addressed by a number of front-line measures such as the replacement of the two 0.312in (7.92mm) MG 15 trainable lateral-firing machine-

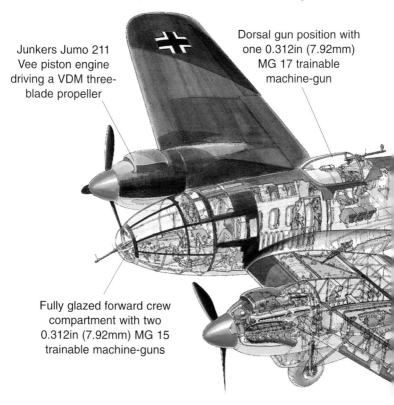

Junkers Jumo 211 Vee piston engine driving a VDM three-blade propeller

Dorsal gun position with one 0.312in (7.92mm) MG 17 trainable machine-gun

Fully glazed forward crew compartment with two 0.312in (7.92mm) MG 15 trainable machine-guns

guns by two 0.312in (7.92mm) MG 81z two-barrel machine-guns in the He 111H-11/R1. The He 111H-11/R2 was another front-line conversion, in this instance with a glider-towing attachment.

He 111H-12: Appearing early in 1943 and lacking the ventral gondola of all earlier He 111H models, the He 111H-12 was planned as a specialised platform for the carriage and launch of two Henschel Hs 293A air-to-surface missiles. The aeroplane carried the missiles under the inner parts of the wing, and there was an operator position in the nose; the control system – whose impulses were transmitted by radio to the released missile via the FuG 203b Kehl III transmitter system – was installed in the dorsal gun position. Only a few aircraft were produced, and it is thought that they were not used operationally.

He 111H-14: This was a pathfinder development of the He 111H-10 with special radio equipment for use by Kampfgeschwader 40 in its anti-shipping role over the eastern part of the Atlantic Ocean, but 20 of the aircraft were modified before delivery to units on the Eastern Front

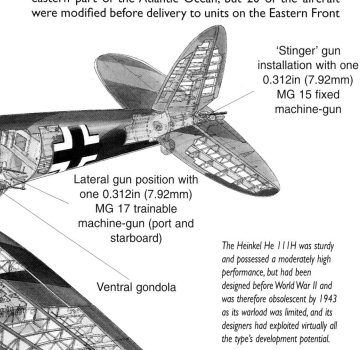

'Stinger' gun installation with one 0.312in (7.92mm) MG 15 fixed machine-gun

Lateral gun position with one 0.312in (7.92mm) MG 17 trainable machine-gun (port and starboard)

Ventral gondola

The Heinkel He 111H was sturdy and possessed a moderately high performance, but had been designed before World War II and was therefore obsolescent by 1943 as its warload was limited, and its designers had exploited virtually all the type's development potential.

as He 111H-14/R2 machines with the special radio equipment removed and a glider-towing attachment added.

He 111H-16: If the He 111H-3 and He 111H-6 were regarded as the first and second definitive models of the He 111H series, the He 111H-16 was the third model and in fact preceded a number of ostensibly earlier models. The He 111H-16 was a development of the He 111H-6 with a powerplant of two Jumo 211F-2 engines and the host of individually small but cumulatively important changes that had been introduced piecemeal on a number of earlier variants. The defensive armament and armour were those of the He 111H-11, and provision was made for a number of different disposable armament arrangements.

Provision was also made for the addition of three *Rüstsätze* (field conversion sets) to provide the He 111H-16/R1 with an electrically operated dorsal turret carrying one 0.51in (13mm) MG 131 machine-gun, the He 111H-16/R2 with a boom-type glider towing attachment, and the He 111H-16/R3 with additional armour protection to operate in the pathfinder role with a reduced weapons load.

He 111H-18: This was a nocturnal pathfinder based on the He 111H-16/R3 but with the special radio equipment of the He 111H-14.

He 111H-20: Although the He 111H had been planned as a bomber, the demands of operations on the Eastern Front had meant that many of the aircraft had been pressed into alternative transport and glider-tug service during the first half of 1942. This capability was reflected later in the same year by the introduction of the He 111H-20, which was a development of the He 111H-16 optimised for adaptability in four main subvariants: the He 111H-20/R1 was a paratroop transport with a crew of three and provision for 16 paratroops who used a ventral jump hatch and could receive equipment dropped to them in two 1,764lb (800kg) externally carried supply containers; the He 111H-20/R2 was a freighter and glider tug with a crew of five including the gunner for the electrically operated dorsal turret armed with a 0.51in (13mm) MG 131 trainable machine-gun; the He 111H-20/R3 was a night bomber with provision for a 4,409lb (2,000kg) weapons load carried on external racks and a defensive armament of three 0.51in (13mm) MG 131 trainable machine-guns in the nose, dorsal and ventral positions plus two 0.312in (7.92mm) MG 81z trainable two-barrel machine-guns in the two beam positions; and the He IIIH-20/R4 was a night harassment bomber with provision for a disposable load of twenty 110lb (50kg) SC50 bombs carried externally.

He IIIH-21: This model signalled the introduction of an uprated powerplant in the form of two Junkers Jumo 213E-1 inverted-Vee piston engines each rated at 1,750hp (1,305kW) for take-off and 1,320hp (984kW) at 31,990ft (9,750m), allowing the maximum weapons load to be increased to 6,614lb (3,000kg) at a maximum take-off weight of 35,273lb (16,000kg). The airframe was basically that of the He IIIH-20/R3 with a measure of local strengthening, and as a result of delays in the delivery of the Jumo 213 engine, the first 22 machines were completed with a powerplant of two Jumo 211F engines equipped with turbochargers for improved high-altitude performance. The definitive model entered service in the late summer of 1944, and possessed a maximum level speed of 259kt (298mph; 480km/h) at optimum altitude.

He IIIH-22: It was clear as the He IIIH-21 was entering service, however, that the days of the He III's utility as a bomber were past, and most aircraft were adapted while still on the production line as airborne launch platforms for the Fieseler Fi 103 pilotless bomb (better known by its Nazi designation of V-)1. The conversion consisted of a carrier under the port or starboard inner wing section, and a number of He IIIH-16 and He IIIH-20 aircraft were also converted to the same standard.

He IIIH-23: The last aircraft of the He IIIH series, completed in the autumn of 1944, were He IIIH-21 warplanes completed to He IIIH-23 standard as saboteur delivery aircraft with accommodation for a demolition team of eight men who were dropped by parachute. The powerplant of this model, of which some were adapted in the field as bombers, was two Jumo 213A-1 engines each rated at 1,776hp (1,324kW) for take-off and 1,600hp (1,193kW) at 18,045ft (5,500m).

The number of He IIIH aircraft built is not known, but certainly amounted to the bulk of the 6,615 aircraft produced between 1939 and 1944 within the overall total of 7,300 or more He III aircraft delivered.